We sincerely hope this grief journal provides you comfort and serves as a gentle reminder that your healing journey begins right here.

Could you take a moment to provide us with a feedback? We highly value your input as it aids us in developing even more impressive products for your enjoyment in the time ahead.

For a closer look at our innovative and appealing product range, please visit our website at amazing-notebooks.com or simply scan the QR code below. We're excited to share our creations with you!

Thank you very much!

Amazing Notebooks

www.amazing-notebooks.com

Copyright © 2023. All rights reserved.

Dear Mom,

I will always love you and miss you with all my heart

...

Until we meet again.

Discover the Power of a Grief Journal

Embracing a grief journal can lead to numerous benefits, tailored to the unique way you use it. Often, individuals find that maintaining such a journal enables them to:

Enhance emotional self-awareness: The act of recording feelings can facilitate a deeper understanding and acknowledgement of the range of emotions you experience.

Decipher thoughts: As you articulate your thoughts on paper, they may become clearer, enabling you to make sense of your inner world.

Experience unfiltered expression: The journal offers a safe space for uncensored and unjudged self-expression, promoting a sense of freedom to share whatever is in your heart.

Safeguard memories: A grief journal serves as a repository for cherished memories, helping you hold on to moments shared with your loved ones.

Reduce stress levels: The process of pouring your heart into a journal can potentially alleviate stress, fostering peace of mind.

Enhance sleep quality: By decluttering your mind before bedtime through journaling, you may find your sleep becoming more restful and rejuvenating.

Track your grief journey: A journal allows you to observe the evolution of your grief over time, fostering introspection and self-awareness.

The practice of maintaining a grief journal inherently promotes a sense of calm and reflection. As you transition your emotions from an internal feeling to tangible words or images on a page, your grief may begin to feel less overwhelming and more navigable.

Mom, my love for you is eternal

My Daily Thoughts:

I will always love you and miss you with all my heart...

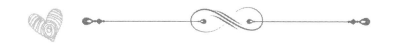

Today, I deeply feel the absence of:

_____

_____

_____

_____

_____

I wish I could tell you:

_____

_____

_____

_____

_____

I am grateful for:

_____

_____

_____

_____

_____

_____

Today, I found it extremely difficult to:

_____

_____

_____

_____

_____

I will always love you and miss you with all my heart...

When burdened by deep pain or despair, I'll:

Grief intensifiers for me are:

My connection with my late mom feels most powerful when:

If I could relive one moment with you, it would be:

I will always love you and miss you with all my heart…

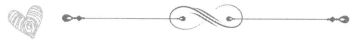

My Daily Thoughts:

_____

_____

_____

_____

_____

_____

_____

_____

_____

_____

_____

_____

_____

_____

_____

_____

I will always love you and miss you with all my heart...

Today, I deeply feel the absence of:

_____
_____
_____
_____

I wish I could tell you:

_____
_____
_____
_____

I am grateful for:

_____
_____
_____
_____
_____

Today, I found it extremely difficult to:

_____
_____
_____
_____

I will always love you and miss you with all my heart...

When burdened by deep pain or despair, I'll:

_____

_____

_____

_____

Grief intensifiers for me are:

_____

_____

_____

_____

My connection with my late mom feels most powerful when:

_____

_____

_____

_____

If I could relive one moment with you, it would be:

_____

_____

_____

_____

I will always love you and miss you with all my heart...

My Daily Thoughts:

I will always love you and miss you with all my heart...

Today, I deeply feel the absence of:

_____

_____

_____

_____

I wish I could tell you:

_____

_____

_____

_____

I am grateful for:

_____

_____

_____

_____

Today, I found it extremely difficult to:

_____

_____

_____

_____

I will always love you and miss you with all my heart…

When burdened by deep pain or despair, I'll:

Grief intensifiers for me are:

My connection with my late mom feels most powerful when:

If I could relive one moment with you, it would be:

I will always love you and miss you with all my heart…

My Daily Thoughts:

I will always love you and miss you with all my heart…

Today, I deeply feel the absence of:

_____

_____

_____

_____

I wish I could tell you:

_____

_____

_____

_____

I am grateful for:

_____

_____

_____

_____

Today, I found it extremely difficult to:

_____

_____

_____

_____

I will always love you and miss you with all my heart…

When burdened by deep pain or despair, I'll:

_____

_____

_____

_____

Grief intensifiers for me are:

_____

_____

_____

_____

My connection with my late mom feels most powerful when:

_____

_____

_____

_____

If I could relive one moment with you, it would be:

_____

_____

_____

_____

I will always love you and miss you with all my heart...

My Daily Thoughts:

I will always love you and miss you with all my heart…

Today, I deeply feel the absence of:

_____

_____

_____

_____

I wish I could tell you:

_____

_____

_____

_____

I am grateful for:

_____

_____

_____

_____

Today, I found it extremely difficult to:

_____

_____

_____

_____

I will always love you and miss you with all my heart…

When burdened by deep pain or despair, I'll:

Grief intensifiers for me are:

My connection with my late mom feels most powerful when:

If I could relive one moment with you, it would be:

I will always love you and miss you with all my heart...

My Daily Thoughts:

I will always love you and miss you with all my heart…

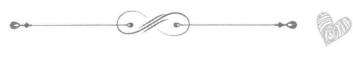

Today, I deeply feel the absence of:

_____
_____
_____
_____
_____

I wish I could tell you:

_____
_____
_____
_____
_____

I am grateful for:

_____
_____
_____
_____
_____

Today, I found it extremely difficult to:

_____
_____
_____
_____

I will always love you and miss you with all my heart…

When burdened by deep pain or despair, I'll:

_____

_____

_____

_____

Grief intensifiers for me are:

_____

_____

_____

_____

My connection with my late mom feels most powerful when:

_____

_____

_____

_____

If I could relive one moment with you, it would be:

_____

_____

_____

_____

I will always love you and miss you with all my heart…

My Daily Thoughts:

I will always love you and miss you with all my heart…

Today, I deeply feel the absence of:

_____

_____

_____

_____

I wish I could tell you:

_____

_____

_____

_____

I am grateful for:

_____

_____

_____

_____

Today, I found it extremely difficult to:

_____

_____

_____

_____

I will always love you and miss you with all my heart…

When burdened by deep pain or despair, I'll:

Grief intensifiers for me are:

My connection with my late mom feels most powerful when:

If I could relive one moment with you, it would be:

I will always love you and miss you with all my heart...

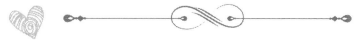

My Daily Thoughts:

I will always love you and miss you with all my heart…

Today, I deeply feel the absence of:

_____
_____
_____
_____
_____

I wish I could tell you:

_____
_____
_____
_____
_____

I am grateful for:

_____
_____
_____
_____
_____

Today, I found it extremely difficult to:

_____
_____
_____
_____

I will always love you and miss you with all my heart...

When burdened by deep pain or despair, I'll:

_____

_____

_____

_____

Grief intensifiers for me are:

_____

_____

_____

_____

My connection with my late mom feels most powerful when:

_____

_____

_____

_____

If I could relive one moment with you, it would be:

_____

_____

_____

_____

I will always love you and miss you with all my heart…

My Daily Thoughts:

I will always love you and miss you with all my heart...

Today, I deeply feel the absence of:

_____
_____
_____
_____

I wish I could tell you:

_____
_____
_____
_____

I am grateful for:

_____
_____
_____
_____
_____

Today, I found it extremely difficult to:

_____
_____
_____
_____

I will always love you and miss you with all my heart...

When burdened by deep pain or despair, I'll:

_____

_____

_____

_____

_____

Grief intensifiers for me are:

_____

_____

_____

_____

_____

My connection with my late mom feels most powerful when:

_____

_____

_____

_____

_____

If I could relive one moment with you, it would be:

_____

_____

_____

_____

I will always love you and miss you with all my heart...

My Daily Thoughts:

I will always love you and miss you with all my heart…

Today, I deeply feel the absence of:

_____

_____

_____

_____

I wish I could tell you:

_____

_____

_____

_____

I am grateful for:

_____

_____

_____

_____

Today, I found it extremely difficult to:

_____

_____

_____

_____

I will always love you and miss you with all my heart…

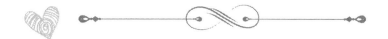

When burdened by deep pain or despair, I'll:

Grief intensifiers for me are:

My connection with my late mom feels most powerful when:

If I could relive one moment with you, it would be:

I will always love you and miss you with all my heart...

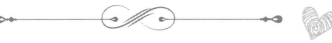

My Daily Thoughts:

I will always love you and miss you with all my heart...

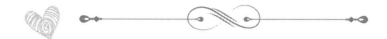

Today, I deeply feel the absence of:

_____
_____
_____
_____
_____

I wish I could tell you:

_____
_____
_____
_____
_____

I am grateful for:

_____
_____
_____
_____
_____

Today, I found it extremely difficult to:

_____
_____
_____
_____

I will always love you and miss you with all my heart…

When burdened by deep pain or despair, I'll:

Grief intensifiers for me are:

My connection with my late mom feels most powerful when:

If I could relive one moment with you, it would be:

I will always love you and miss you with all my heart…

My Daily Thoughts:

I will always love you and miss you with all my heart…

Today, I deeply feel the absence of:

_____
_____
_____
_____
_____

I wish I could tell you:

_____
_____
_____
_____
_____

I am grateful for:

_____
_____
_____
_____
_____

Today, I found it extremely difficult to:

_____
_____
_____
_____
_____

I will always love you and miss you with all my heart...

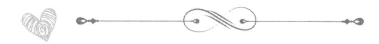

When burdened by deep pain or despair, I'll:

Grief intensifiers for me are:

My connection with my late mom feels most powerful when:

If I could relive one moment with you, it would be:

I will always love you and miss you with all my heart…

My Daily Thoughts:

I will always love you and miss you with all my heart…

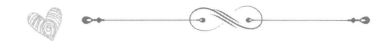

Today, I deeply feel the absence of:

_____

_____

_____

_____

I wish I could tell you:

_____

_____

_____

_____

I am grateful for:

_____

_____

_____

_____

Today, I found it extremely difficult to:

_____

_____

_____

_____

I will always love you and miss you with all my heart…

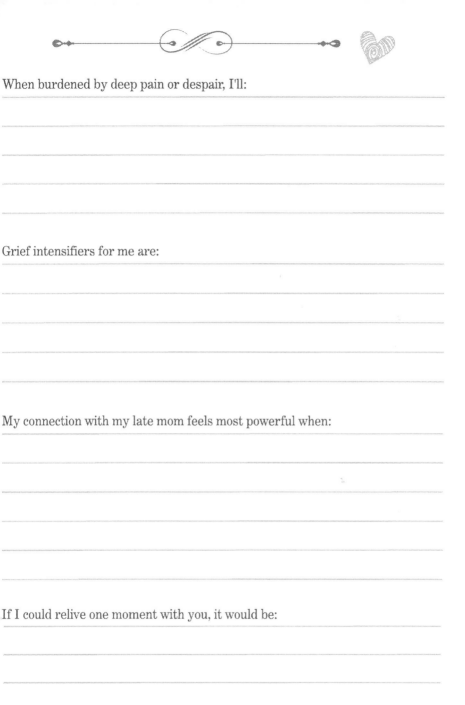

When burdened by deep pain or despair, I'll:

Grief intensifiers for me are:

My connection with my late mom feels most powerful when:

If I could relive one moment with you, it would be:

I will always love you and miss you with all my heart...

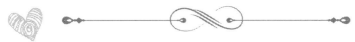

My Daily Thoughts:

I will always love you and miss you with all my heart...

Today, I deeply feel the absence of:

_____
_____
_____
_____
_____

I wish I could tell you:

_____
_____
_____
_____
_____

I am grateful for:

_____
_____
_____
_____
_____

Today, I found it extremely difficult to:

_____
_____
_____
_____

I will always love you and miss you with all my heart…

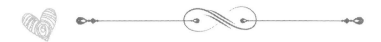

When burdened by deep pain or despair, I'll:

_____

_____

_____

_____

Grief intensifiers for me are:

_____

_____

_____

_____

My connection with my late mom feels most powerful when:

_____

_____

_____

_____

If I could relive one moment with you, it would be:

_____

_____

_____

_____

I will always love you and miss you with all my heart...

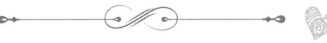

My Daily Thoughts:

I will always love you and miss you with all my heart...

Today, I deeply feel the absence of:

I wish I could tell you:

I am grateful for:

Today, I found it extremely difficult to:

I will always love you and miss you with all my heart…

When burdened by deep pain or despair, I'll:

Grief intensifiers for me are:

My connection with my late mom feels most powerful when:

If I could relive one moment with you, it would be:

I will always love you and miss you with all my heart...

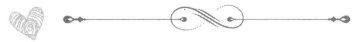

My Daily Thoughts:

I will always love you and miss you with all my heart…

Today, I deeply feel the absence of:

_____
_____
_____
_____
_____

I wish I could tell you:

_____
_____
_____
_____
_____

I am grateful for:

_____
_____
_____
_____
_____

Today, I found it extremely difficult to:

_____
_____
_____
_____

I will always love you and miss you with all my heart…

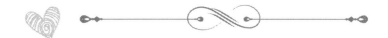

When burdened by deep pain or despair, I'll:

_____

_____

_____

_____

Grief intensifiers for me are:

_____

_____

_____

_____

My connection with my late mom feels most powerful when:

_____

_____

_____

_____

If I could relive one moment with you, it would be:

_____

_____

_____

_____

I will always love you and miss you with all my heart...

My Daily Thoughts:

I will always love you and miss you with all my heart…

Today, I deeply feel the absence of:

I wish I could tell you:

I am grateful for:

Today, I found it extremely difficult to:

I will always love you and miss you with all my heart…

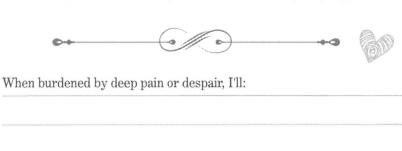

When burdened by deep pain or despair, I'll:

Grief intensifiers for me are:

My connection with my late mom feels most powerful when:

If I could relive one moment with you, it would be:

I will always love you and miss you with all my heart...

My Daily Thoughts:

I will always love you and miss you with all my heart...

Today, I deeply feel the absence of:

_____
_____
_____
_____

I wish I could tell you:

_____
_____
_____
_____

I am grateful for:

_____
_____
_____
_____

Today, I found it extremely difficult to:

_____
_____
_____
_____

I will always love you and miss you with all my heart...

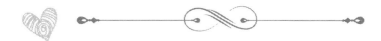

When burdened by deep pain or despair, I'll:

Grief intensifiers for me are:

My connection with my late mom feels most powerful when:

If I could relive one moment with you, it would be:

I will always love you and miss you with all my heart…

My Daily Thoughts:

I will always love you and miss you with all my heart…

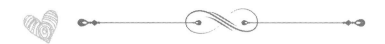

Today, I deeply feel the absence of:

_____

_____

_____

_____

I wish I could tell you:

_____

_____

_____

_____

I am grateful for:

_____

_____

_____

_____

_____

Today, I found it extremely difficult to:

_____

_____

_____

_____

I will always love you and miss you with all my heart…

When burdened by deep pain or despair, I'll:

_____

_____

_____

_____

_____

Grief intensifiers for me are:

_____

_____

_____

_____

_____

My connection with my late mom feels most powerful when:

_____

_____

_____

_____

_____

If I could relive one moment with you, it would be:

_____

_____

_____

_____

_____

I will always love you and miss you with all my heart...

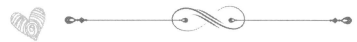

My Daily Thoughts:

I will always love you and miss you with all my heart…

Today, I deeply feel the absence of:

_____
_____
_____
_____
_____

I wish I could tell you:

_____
_____
_____
_____
_____

I am grateful for:

_____
_____
_____
_____
_____
_____

Today, I found it extremely difficult to:

_____
_____
_____
_____
_____

I will always love you and miss you with all my heart…

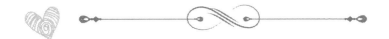

When burdened by deep pain or despair, I'll:

_____

_____

_____

_____

Grief intensifiers for me are:

_____

_____

_____

_____

My connection with my late mom feels most powerful when:

_____

_____

_____

_____

If I could relive one moment with you, it would be:

_____

_____

_____

_____

I will always love you and miss you with all my heart…

My Daily Thoughts:

I will always love you and miss you with all my heart...

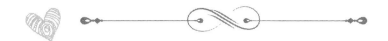

Today, I deeply feel the absence of:

_____

_____

_____

_____

I wish I could tell you:

_____

_____

_____

_____

I am grateful for:

_____

_____

_____

_____

Today, I found it extremely difficult to:

_____

_____

_____

_____

I will always love you and miss you with all my heart...

When burdened by deep pain or despair, I'll:

_____

_____

_____

_____

_____

Grief intensifiers for me are:

_____

_____

_____

_____

_____

My connection with my late mom feels most powerful when:

_____

_____

_____

_____

_____

If I could relive one moment with you, it would be:

_____

_____

_____

_____

I will always love you and miss you with all my heart...

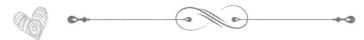

My Daily Thoughts:

I will always love you and miss you with all my heart...

Today, I deeply feel the absence of:

_____
_____
_____
_____

I wish I could tell you:

_____
_____
_____
_____

I am grateful for:

_____
_____
_____
_____

Today, I found it extremely difficult to:

_____
_____
_____
_____

I will always love you and miss you with all my heart...

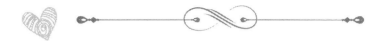

When burdened by deep pain or despair, I'll:

_____

_____

_____

_____

Grief intensifiers for me are:

_____

_____

_____

_____

My connection with my late mom feels most powerful when:

_____

_____

_____

_____

If I could relive one moment with you, it would be:

_____

_____

_____

_____

I will always love you and miss you with all my heart…

My Daily Thoughts:

I will always love you and miss you with all my heart...

Today, I deeply feel the absence of:

_____

_____

_____

_____

I wish I could tell you:

_____

_____

_____

_____

I am grateful for:

_____

_____

_____

_____

Today, I found it extremely difficult to:

_____

_____

_____

_____

I will always love you and miss you with all my heart…

When burdened by deep pain or despair, I'll:

Grief intensifiers for me are:

My connection with my late mom feels most powerful when:

If I could relive one moment with you, it would be:

I will always love you and miss you with all my heart…

My Daily Thoughts:

I will always love you and miss you with all my heart...

Today, I deeply feel the absence of:

_____

_____

_____

_____

_____

I wish I could tell you:

_____

_____

_____

_____

_____

I am grateful for:

_____

_____

_____

_____

_____

Today, I found it extremely difficult to:

_____

_____

_____

_____

_____

I will always love you and miss you with all my heart…

When burdened by deep pain or despair, I'll:

_____

_____

_____

_____

_____

Grief intensifiers for me are:

_____

_____

_____

_____

_____

My connection with my late mom feels most powerful when:

_____

_____

_____

_____

_____

_____

If I could relive one moment with you, it would be:

_____

_____

_____

_____

_____

I will always love you and miss you with all my heart…

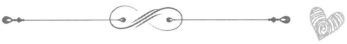

My Daily Thoughts:

I will always love you and miss you with all my heart...

Today, I deeply feel the absence of:

_____

_____

_____

_____

I wish I could tell you:

_____

_____

_____

_____

I am grateful for:

_____

_____

_____

_____

Today, I found it extremely difficult to:

_____

_____

_____

_____

I will always love you and miss you with all my heart...

When burdened by deep pain or despair, I'll:

Grief intensifiers for me are:

My connection with my late mom feels most powerful when:

If I could relive one moment with you, it would be:

I will always love you and miss you with all my heart...

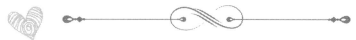

My Daily Thoughts:

I will always love you and miss you with all my heart…

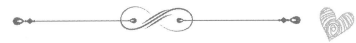

Today, I deeply feel the absence of:

_____

_____

_____

_____

_____

I wish I could tell you:

_____

_____

_____

_____

_____

I am grateful for:

_____

_____

_____

_____

_____

Today, I found it extremely difficult to:

_____

_____

_____

_____

_____

I will always love you and miss you with all my heart…

When burdened by deep pain or despair, I'll:

Grief intensifiers for me are:

My connection with my late mom feels most powerful when:

If I could relive one moment with you, it would be:

I will always love you and miss you with all my heart…

My Daily Thoughts:

I will always love you and miss you with all my heart…

Today, I deeply feel the absence of:

_____
_____
_____
_____

I wish I could tell you:

_____
_____
_____
_____

I am grateful for:

_____
_____
_____
_____

Today, I found it extremely difficult to:

_____
_____
_____
_____

I will always love you and miss you with all my heart…

When burdened by deep pain or despair, I'll:

Grief intensifiers for me are:

My connection with my late mom feels most powerful when:

If I could relive one moment with you, it would be:

I will always love you and miss you with all my heart...

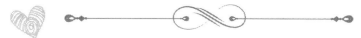

My Daily Thoughts:

I will always love you and miss you with all my heart...

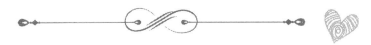

Today, I deeply feel the absence of:

_____

_____

_____

_____

_____

I wish I could tell you:

_____

_____

_____

_____

_____

I am grateful for:

_____

_____

_____

_____

_____

_____

Today, I found it extremely difficult to:

_____

_____

_____

_____

_____

I will always love you and miss you with all my heart…

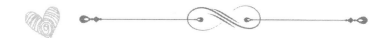

When burdened by deep pain or despair, I'll:

_____
_____
_____
_____
_____

Grief intensifiers for me are:

_____
_____
_____
_____
_____

My connection with my late mom feels most powerful when:

_____
_____
_____
_____
_____

If I could relive one moment with you, it would be:

_____
_____
_____
_____

I will always love you and miss you with all my heart…

My Daily Thoughts:

I will always love you and miss you with all my heart…

Today, I deeply feel the absence of:

_____
_____
_____
_____
_____

I wish I could tell you:

_____
_____
_____
_____
_____

I am grateful for:

_____
_____
_____
_____
_____

Today, I found it extremely difficult to:

_____
_____
_____
_____
_____

I will always love you and miss you with all my heart…

When burdened by deep pain or despair, I'll:

Grief intensifiers for me are:

My connection with my late mom feels most powerful when:

If I could relive one moment with you, it would be:

I will always love you and miss you with all my heart...

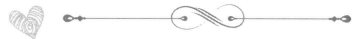

My Daily Thoughts:

I will always love you and miss you with all my heart…

Today, I deeply feel the absence of:

_____

_____

_____

_____

I wish I could tell you:

_____

_____

_____

_____

I am grateful for:

_____

_____

_____

_____

Today, I found it extremely difficult to:

_____

_____

_____

_____

I will always love you and miss you with all my heart…

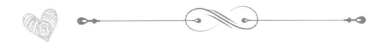

When burdened by deep pain or despair, I'll:

_____

_____

_____

_____

Grief intensifiers for me are:

_____

_____

_____

_____

My connection with my late mom feels most powerful when:

_____

_____

_____

_____

_____

If I could relive one moment with you, it would be:

_____

_____

_____

_____

I will always love you and miss you with all my heart…

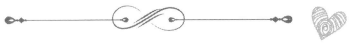

My Daily Thoughts:

I will always love you and miss you with all my heart...

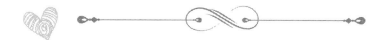

Today, I deeply feel the absence of:

_____

_____

_____

_____

I wish I could tell you:

_____

_____

_____

_____

I am grateful for:

_____

_____

_____

_____

_____

Today, I found it extremely difficult to:

_____

_____

_____

_____

I will always love you and miss you with all my heart…

When burdened by deep pain or despair, I'll:

Grief intensifiers for me are:

My connection with my late mom feels most powerful when:

If I could relive one moment with you, it would be:

I will always love you and miss you with all my heart...

My Daily Thoughts:

I will always love you and miss you with all my heart...

Today, I deeply feel the absence of:

_____

_____

_____

_____

I wish I could tell you:

_____

_____

_____

_____

I am grateful for:

_____

_____

_____

_____

Today, I found it extremely difficult to:

_____

_____

_____

_____

I will always love you and miss you with all my heart…

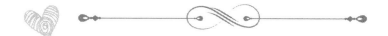

When burdened by deep pain or despair, I'll:

_____

_____

_____

_____

Grief intensifiers for me are:

_____

_____

_____

_____

My connection with my late mom feels most powerful when:

_____

_____

_____

_____

If I could relive one moment with you, it would be:

_____

_____

_____

_____

I will always love you and miss you with all my heart…

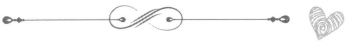

My Daily Thoughts:

I will always love you and miss you with all my heart…

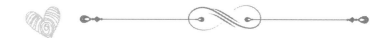

Today, I deeply feel the absence of:

_____

_____

_____

_____

I wish I could tell you:

_____

_____

_____

_____

I am grateful for:

_____

_____

_____

_____

Today, I found it extremely difficult to:

_____

_____

_____

_____

I will always love you and miss you with all my heart...

When burdened by deep pain or despair, I'll:

Grief intensifiers for me are:

My connection with my late mom feels most powerful when:

If I could relive one moment with you, it would be:

I will always love you and miss you with all my heart...

My Daily Thoughts:

I will always love you and miss you with all my heart…

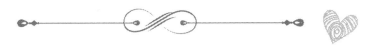

Today, I deeply feel the absence of:

_____
_____
_____
_____
_____

I wish I could tell you:

_____
_____
_____
_____
_____

I am grateful for:

_____
_____
_____
_____
_____

Today, I found it extremely difficult to:

_____
_____
_____
_____
_____

I will always love you and miss you with all my heart…

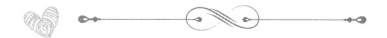

When burdened by deep pain or despair, I'll:

_____

_____

_____

_____

Grief intensifiers for me are:

_____

_____

_____

_____

My connection with my late mom feels most powerful when:

_____

_____

_____

_____

If I could relive one moment with you, it would be:

_____

_____

_____

_____

I will always love you and miss you with all my heart...

My Daily Thoughts:

I will always love you and miss you with all my heart...

Today, I deeply feel the absence of:

_____

_____

_____

_____

I wish I could tell you:

_____

_____

_____

_____

I am grateful for:

_____

_____

_____

_____

Today, I found it extremely difficult to:

_____

_____

_____

_____

I will always love you and miss you with all my heart...

When burdened by deep pain or despair, I'll:

_____

_____

_____

_____

_____

Grief intensifiers for me are:

_____

_____

_____

_____

_____

My connection with my late mom feels most powerful when:

_____

_____

_____

_____

_____

If I could relive one moment with you, it would be:

_____

_____

_____

_____

_____

I will always love you and miss you with all my heart...

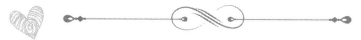

My Daily Thoughts:

I will always love you and miss you with all my heart…

Today, I deeply feel the absence of:

_____

_____

_____

_____

I wish I could tell you:

_____

_____

_____

_____

I am grateful for:

_____

_____

_____

_____

Today, I found it extremely difficult to:

_____

_____

_____

_____

I will always love you and miss you with all my heart…

When burdened by deep pain or despair, I'll:

_____

_____

_____

_____

Grief intensifiers for me are:

_____

_____

_____

_____

My connection with my late mom feels most powerful when:

_____

_____

_____

_____

If I could relive one moment with you, it would be:

_____

_____

_____

_____

I will always love you and miss you with all my heart…

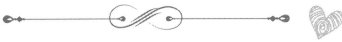

My Daily Thoughts:

I will always love you and miss you with all my heart…

Today, I deeply feel the absence of:

_____
_____
_____
_____
_____

I wish I could tell you:

_____
_____
_____
_____
_____

I am grateful for:

_____
_____
_____
_____
_____

Today, I found it extremely difficult to:

_____
_____
_____
_____
_____

I will always love you and miss you with all my heart...

When burdened by deep pain or despair, I'll:

_____
_____
_____
_____

Grief intensifiers for me are:

_____
_____
_____
_____

My connection with my late mom feels most powerful when:

_____
_____
_____
_____

If I could relive one moment with you, it would be:

_____
_____
_____
_____

I will always love you and miss you with all my heart…

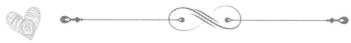

My Daily Thoughts:

I will always love you and miss you with all my heart…

Today, I deeply feel the absence of:

I wish I could tell you:

I am grateful for:

Today, I found it extremely difficult to:

I will always love you and miss you with all my heart…

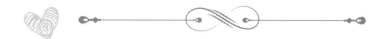

When burdened by deep pain or despair, I'll:

_____

_____

_____

_____

Grief intensifiers for me are:

_____

_____

_____

_____

My connection with my late mom feels most powerful when:

_____

_____

_____

_____

_____

If I could relive one moment with you, it would be:

_____

_____

_____

_____

I will always love you and miss you with all my heart…

My Daily Thoughts:

I will always love you and miss you with all my heart…

Today, I deeply feel the absence of:

_____

_____

_____

_____

_____

I wish I could tell you:

_____

_____

_____

_____

_____

I am grateful for:

_____

_____

_____

_____

_____

Today, I found it extremely difficult to:

_____

_____

_____

_____

I will always love you and miss you with all my heart…

When burdened by deep pain or despair, I'll:

Grief intensifiers for me are:

My connection with my late mom feels most powerful when:

If I could relive one moment with you, it would be:

I will always love you and miss you with all my heart…

My Daily Thoughts:

_____

_____

_____

_____

_____

_____

_____

_____

_____

_____

_____

_____

_____

_____

_____

_____

_____

_____

_____

_____

_____

_____

I will always love you and miss you with all my heart…

Today, I deeply feel the absence of:

_____

_____

_____

_____

I wish I could tell you:

_____

_____

_____

_____

I am grateful for:

_____

_____

_____

_____

Today, I found it extremely difficult to:

_____

_____

_____

_____

I will always love you and miss you with all my heart…

When burdened by deep pain or despair, I'll:

Grief intensifiers for me are:

My connection with my late mom feels most powerful when:

If I could relive one moment with you, it would be:

I will always love you and miss you with all my heart…

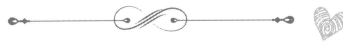

My Daily Thoughts:

I will always love you and miss you with all my heart…

Today, I deeply feel the absence of:

_____

_____

_____

_____

_____

I wish I could tell you:

_____

_____

_____

_____

_____

I am grateful for:

_____

_____

_____

_____

_____

_____

Today, I found it extremely difficult to:

_____

_____

_____

_____

I will always love you and miss you with all my heart…

When burdened by deep pain or despair, I'll:

Grief intensifiers for me are:

My connection with my late mom feels most powerful when:

If I could relive one moment with you, it would be:

I will always love you and miss you with all my heart...

My Daily Thoughts:

_____

_____

_____

_____

_____

_____

_____

_____

_____

_____

_____

_____

_____

_____

_____

_____

_____

_____

_____

_____

I will always love you and miss you with all my heart…

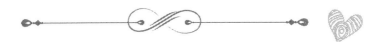

Today, I deeply feel the absence of:

_____
_____
_____
_____
_____

I wish I could tell you:

_____
_____
_____
_____
_____

I am grateful for:

_____
_____
_____
_____
_____
_____

Today, I found it extremely difficult to:

_____
_____
_____
_____
_____

I will always love you and miss you with all my heart…

When burdened by deep pain or despair, I'll:

Grief intensifiers for me are:

My connection with my late mom feels most powerful when:

If I could relive one moment with you, it would be:

I will always love you and miss you with all my heart...

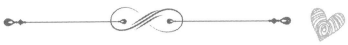

My Daily Thoughts:

_____

_____

_____

_____

_____

_____

_____

_____

_____

_____

_____

_____

_____

_____

_____

_____

_____

_____

_____

I will always love you and miss you with all my heart…

Today, I deeply feel the absence of:

_____

_____

_____

_____

I wish I could tell you:

_____

_____

_____

_____

I am grateful for:

_____

_____

_____

_____

_____

Today, I found it extremely difficult to:

_____

_____

_____

_____

I will always love you and miss you with all my heart…

When burdened by deep pain or despair, I'll:

_____
_____
_____
_____
_____

Grief intensifiers for me are:

_____
_____
_____
_____
_____
_____

My connection with my late mom feels most powerful when:

_____
_____
_____
_____
_____
_____

If I could relive one moment with you, it would be:

_____
_____
_____
_____

I will always love you and miss you with all my heart...

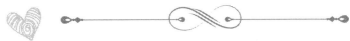

My Daily Thoughts:

_____

_____

_____

_____

_____

_____

_____

_____

_____

_____

_____

_____

_____

_____

_____

_____

_____

_____

_____

_____

_____

_____

I will always love you and miss you with all my heart…

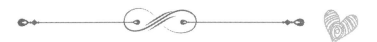

Today, I deeply feel the absence of:

_____
_____
_____
_____
_____

I wish I could tell you:

_____
_____
_____
_____
_____

I am grateful for:

_____
_____
_____
_____
_____

Today, I found it extremely difficult to:

_____
_____
_____
_____

I will always love you and miss you with all my heart...

When burdened by deep pain or despair, I'll:

_____

_____

_____

_____

Grief intensifiers for me are:

_____

_____

_____

_____

My connection with my late mom feels most powerful when:

_____

_____

_____

_____

If I could relive one moment with you, it would be:

_____

_____

_____

_____

I will always love you and miss you with all my heart…

My Daily Thoughts:

I will always love you and miss you with all my heart…

Today, I deeply feel the absence of:

_____

_____

_____

_____

I wish I could tell you:

_____

_____

_____

_____

I am grateful for:

_____

_____

_____

_____

Today, I found it extremely difficult to:

_____

_____

_____

_____

I will always love you and miss you with all my heart…

When burdened by deep pain or despair, I'll:

Grief intensifiers for me are:

My connection with my late mom feels most powerful when:

If I could relive one moment with you, it would be:

I will always love you and miss you with all my heart…

We trust that you'll find value in this journal, and always keep in mind that it's your journey.

Could you take a moment to provide us with a feedback? We highly value your input as it aids us in developing even more impressive products for your enjoyment in the time ahead.

For a closer look at our innovative and appealing product range, please visit our website at amazing-notebooks.com or simply scan the QR code below. We're excited to share our creations with you!

Thank you very much!

Amazing Notebooks

www.amazing-notebooks.com

Made in the USA
Columbia, SC
07 February 2024

28222b39-3258-425b-ae45-18016892e14eR01